TO A NEW ERA

Other Books by Joanna Fuhrman

Freud in Brooklyn

Ugh Ugh Ocean

Moraine

Pageant

The Emotive Function

The Year of Yellow Butterflies

To a New Era

Joanna Fuhrman

Hanging Loose Press,
Brooklyn, New York

Published by Hanging Loose Press, 231 Wyckoff Street, Brooklyn, New York 11217-2208.

www.hangingloosepress.com

Printed in the United States of America 10 9 8 7 6 5 4 3 2 1

Cover art: "We Try Hard to Prove We Are Not Criminals" by Julie Peppito
Cover/Book design: Nanako Inoue

Hanging Loose thanks the Literature Program of the New York State Council on the Arts for a grant in support of the publication of this book.

ISBN: 978-1-934909-69-0

TABLE OF CONTENTS

CONTENTS

For Noah and Sandra Fuhrman

"A bridge is a dangerous neighborhood."

— *David Shapiro*

"But where danger threatens / That which saves from it also grows."

—*Friedrich Hölderlin*, translated by *Michael Hamburger*

To a New Era

If history is a circle, how long
will it take to lick the lollipop
and get to the empty core?

Could there be a sentient creature
sleeping in its center?
A Tootsie Pop Mermaid of History?

If so, wake her up!

Feed her the ghostly bodies
created by twitterbots and conspiracy tambourines.

Let her destroy them with her split tongue!

Sing to her of babies yet
to know the meaning of disgust.

Teach her to kick, to run on her fishy tail
and karate chop the gears of time,
until they resemble steam-punk-frayed metal wings.

Here the radius of the sun
can meet the radical endpoint
of our hope, buttermilk, dolphin dreams,
hot-air balloons, oceanic longing and/or weeping
and start again
as pure immaterial possibility.

FOSTER AVENUE

The B Train

feels like a crumpled fedora sliding
through the chattering tunnels of the damned,

and the rails' clanging almost
completely covers the folksong

of the migrant accordionist, but it is
love for you with your cubist profiles

of shattering chandeliers
that illuminates my life.

I'm thankful to you all:
the young lovers in the corner,

he in ripped corduroys, she
modeling the day-glo uniform

of a fast-food chicken empire,
and the mini old lady balancing

a massive aqua ball gown
in a plastic dry-cleaning shell.

In these moments I know
that the boy with the furrowed

baseball cap is writing poetry
on his cell, and the toddler

smiling with all seven of her
best teeth—I am sure

her joy is transmittable, like
those microbes crashing

towards me from the tourist's
insubordinate sneeze.

The Adjunct Commuter

I fell asleep on a bus and when I woke
I was the bus: lumbering, mythic, dumb.

My superego had been replaced with an ornery
driver who cursed if anyone asked on what street

the bus would turn. My unquantifiable desire
was now a red throbbing steering wheel.

Everyone who mattered rode in the back.
My mother held an empty coffee cup

full of disobedient air. My father wandered
the aisles, looking for his childhood stutter.

My husband was reading a novel about
the future where everyone turned into a bus.

My past self was swinging a knife at a periwinkle
simulacrum of her youth. Fear wore a yellow trench coat,

took embarrassing pictures of sleeping passengers
to post online. Did the city own the bus, or did the bus

own the city? I had at least a million buses flowing
through my valves. This was a kind of power, but also

a kind of failure. I wanted to embrace it, to make
my failure so big it would swallow the whole street,

replace the city with another city where everyone was also
a bus— a failure or a bus. Instead, the light changed.

Children with backpacks bigger than their bodies crammed
my aisles, then left. An old couple held hands, made jokes

about the teenagers falling out of their baggy jeans
or squeezed into aqua spandex leggings.

Once a woman with a dress decorated with Op Art eyes
kicked a stranger's cellphone-wielding ass out the door.

Everyone inside the bus laughed, and I laughed too,
pushing the laughing smoke out of my old pipes.

Years later, I had forgotten I was ever *not* a bus. Each night
I slept in the warm comfort of the city's old garage.

I was happy writing poetry in retreaded miles, content
with the familiar smell of gasoline and weak bodega coffee.

Are We Having Fun Yet?

Every year, our belief in the future is more defunded.
We try embracing the spaces in austerity's lace, funneling
chaos into kaleidoscopic slivers, into funky
prepositions bumping their hopes against malfunctioning
doors, traveling skyward on rickety funiculars
in pre-gentrified cities. If we are fundamentally

timeless, can we still be damaged by time? Fundamentally
we morph like financial products not yet defunded,
delicate enough to balance on the roof of a funicular.
Washing the debris of the past through a funnel,
we find joy in the smell of malfunction,
creeping through consciousness like funky

caterpillars. Is this shifting the reason today's funky
music sounds like yesterday's dirge? Fundamentally
we are itinerant nitwits malfunctioning
in rumpus rooms. Dimwitted and defunded,
we scurry through cities in funnel-
adorned fedoras, hijack trackless funiculars

helicoptering into funiculars—
not really crashing, more like funky
lovemaking than disaster. We funnel
the debris to create worlds, fundamental
as strangers to our defunded
metropolis. We wait for a malfunction.

Who doesn't love juicy malfunctions,
the way they hang off the back of the funicular,
debris sticking to tendrils? Proud yet defunded,
we don't care about propriety anymore. Our funky
scent drips over our nation, new and fundamentally
free, like space and time departing a funnel

and drifting apart. No longer needing to funnel
meaning from the objects that malfunction,
we unleash our butterflies into fundamentals,
waiting before we exit this inter-atomic funicular,
celebrating the spaces between teeth, the funky
breath of abject freedom. We embrace defunding.

Fundamentally can't we do more than funnel
our hope into malfunctioning vessels? Defeated? Defunded?
Oh, funk it—even a broken funicular can be fun.

Song of Flatbush

Yes, I may crash into my sixties still schlepping heavy
laundry down two flights of stairs and seven and a half

unevenly sidewalked blocks, but I have eaten
pickled raisins four times in three days,

and met poets from 36 states (and a good percent
of them were kind), and walked almost eight miles

each birth of spring, and eavesdropped on a young girl
drawing a picture of a baby pacifier with a face

(sucking on a smaller pacifier), and written poetry
on every mode of public transportation, and baked

a chocolate cake made of chickpeas, and made love
in multiple cheapish hotels, and talked to close friends

on both landlines and cells, and been so tired from teaching
in four different places to three different ages in two days

that I felt an elation as unbridled as love unsheathed
from its jacket of language, creeping outward in every

direction, clarifying like the feeling of thinking, like
the texture of living in magnified, temporary air.

Why Can't Middle Age Be Like Childhood, but with Sex, Liquor and Hipper Boots?

Some days all I need to be happy is a subway seat
and a Diet Dr Pepper. Other days I'm waiting

for the fog to spell out my name. (It never happens.)
I want to believe in the green spaces between my emotions,

that mythical quietness where baby ducks waddle
and hide cloud babies under their wings,

but then anger shows up again, dressed like
an old-fashioned nun from a comic book,

carrying a yapping chihuahua in her black
patent handbag. She wants to punch the sunset,

wants the moonlight to whiten her teeth,
but all the groaning in her bones gets in the way.

Why can't middle age be like that TV show
where the ending comes at the beginning?

Everyone knows it's going to be tragic, so why not
show that first? Then we can focus on the love story—

the center of the desk drawer's wrapped truffle,
the bodega kitten's upstretched off-white neck.

Foster Avenue

Sitting in the bathtub
with the window open,
I can hear from across
the Flatbush alley
the primal scream of what
I assume is a toddler
or young child.
          He is yelling
in an unwavering, unending spurt.
It's like a wound with a mouth
and megaphone.
          He could be crying
about the loss of a father,
or the collapsing of the universe.
I don't know what it is
that's causing the unearthing
of such deep sadness,
          but I feel like it could be
emerging from me, emanating
from some other version of myself,
a Joanna more connected
to her own sadness than I am.

Finally, after a few minutes,
his mother translates
his screams.
          "Oh, you want *lemonade*,"
and he's quiet,
and the whole street is quiet,
as it's never been before,
even the banging radiator pipes
are quiet
and the sparrows

with their angry chirps are quiet,
          and I wish
my own unexpressed
weeping could be quelled
with something
as simple
as the promise of a glass
of lemonade, so
          I imagine that glass
of lemonade, pithy,
yellow, swirled
with sugar
in a frosted glass.

Breaker

A black wave surrounds me in slow motion.
I am dry, warm inside a claw-foot bathtub
carved from an idea of art. The black wave
is the whole ocean, humming a single note.

I am dry, warm inside a claw-foot bathtub.
I wonder, how can I be safe when the wave
is the whole ocean? Humming a single note,
my mind is the ocean and I am safe within it.

I wonder, how can I be safe when the wave
is larger than the shore and swallows the tub?
My mind is the ocean and I am safe within it.
I smell another wave, years away. The water

is larger than the shore and swallows the tub
forged out of thinking and solid as bone.
I smell another wave, years away. The water
is the size of everything I thought was the world.

Forged out of thinking and solid as bone,
the bathtub is a halo, keeping me safe. The wave
is the size of everything I thought was the world.
It's just a wave, and waves disappear.

The bathtub is a halo. Keeping me safe: the wave,
now just an idea. I breathe in the clean air.
It's just a wave, and waves disappear.
I float on the air inside a giant bathtub.

Now just an idea, I breathe in the clean air.
A black wave surrounds me in slow motion.
I float on the air inside a giant bathtub.
Carved from an idea of art, the black wave.

Why the Symmetry of a Bagel Is an Atheist Prayer

My coffee tastes like water,
and my bodega bagel
envies the honestness of a roll.

So do I.

Some people are all
about the now, now.

I'm all about
the how how.

There's something
in the past, a ghost purple
who-are-you

lurking between
the shoulders of city people
that makes me
want to stay.

And who else besides us
is able to feel the eyes
of the three-legged

deli cat looking up
a stranger's pant leg,
right into her soul?

To a Broken Window or a Future Self

(July 2020)

I used to think all poetry was written
for a better version of myself. I'd imagine her,
walking home beside the moon riding
its fuchsia tricycle through Newkirk Plaza,
past children dressed in their best white for Eid,
playfully chasing each other in circles.
The other me was full of "Joannaness": a quality
often translated as "the ability to be 1,000 percent herself
without having the faintest idea who she was or is,
or where the nexus—of wild hair meets wild joking
meets octopi-like feeling—might begin or end."
  Now I think Joannaness might be
something less like an ocean in a bathtub and more
like a banal dream, the kind where you are
shopping for a blender at a department store,
but when you wake up all you can remember
about the dream is the price of the object you forgot
to buy. Instead of writing to my better self, I need
to start writing to my future self, imagine who
I'll be when all my hair is gray, my parents dead,
the books I've written out of print. Will future
Joanna still see her childhood poems circling
the ether like drunk angels crashing their cloud
mobiles into post-literature, or will their metaphors
be forgotten, recycled into advertisements for
security systems? Will future Joanna still love
strong iced coffee, installation art and gardenias?
Or will she be the kind of woman who spends
all day in the streets, trying to dig up
a Brooklyn that's already gone?

Whiskers

Bob's pandemic beard is the new member
of our household. He pets it as if there were
a kitten crawling across his chin. I say,
"How come *you* can have a beard-cat but
you won't let me get a real cat?" A beard-cat
is no use as a cat—it doesn't jump for the ragged
tips of peacock feathers, doesn't wake me up
with its wet nose, doesn't crawl on my chest
and purr when I hear from my dad that my mom
in the Florida hospital isn't getting better.
The beard-cat doesn't even meow or growl
or pounce at crows at the window. As I pout,
the beard-cat jumps off Bob's face and swan dives
into what I imagine is a moment in our post-COVID
future—a silver-lit evening where we are munching
shrimp tacos under the multicolored garlands
of a Mexican café (in Mexico, perhaps), or where
we are huddling with tourists admiring
Sophie Taeuber-Arp's dancing Dada dolls
at the new MOMA. As we worry about everything—
all the past and future deaths ricocheting off
the decapitated statues of disjointed piazzas,
all the lost possibilities of lips grazing lips,
the missed handshakes and hugs free-falling
into intergalactic tunnels—the beard-cat is
pirouetting on the rips in time between now
and then. It weaves a flag out of the threads it
has pulled from continuity, tries to surrender
to a dragon with its flame blistering the stratosphere.
Each night, the beard-cat rips the walls off
our bedroom, replacing them with a mass
of undulating orange paws.

Dear beard-cat, please
forgive me for not loving you enough when all
you were trying to do was mark time, to provide
a little salt-and-pepper-colored hair-tainment
to a confined middle-aged couple. When you
are finally ready to say goodbye, promise you'll
allow me to stroke your pale tendrils one last time.
Let me decorate your rough fur with marigolds.

I've Got a Cell Phone in My Pocket, Instead of a Heart

(*October 2018*)

The sign says *False Alarms Kill*
          not *Kill the False Alarm*

On the sidewalk, a pile of croutons
but no birds pecking at them

A winter tree with thin branches sloping down
          reminds me of a singer in a hair band

Do people still know what hair bands are?

On Newkirk, a woman pushes a grocery cart
full of who knows what

An ambulette drives by   Who invented the word
ambulette? Did they mean it to be so cute?

The garbage cans are in a chain gang
We all need heavy-metal locks these days

On the ground, a small hand-painted sign
          Take time with my god

In a parked SUV
a man is laughing to himself

Is he laughing at me? Why did I leave
the apartment in my rainbow gym leggings,
dirty puffer coat and zero makeup?

No, he's just talking on his cell

The sparrows sound like they're using bullhorns

In 2018, even the birds need to protest

I turn a corner
            and I'm in houseland

the fancy block Bob likes to pretend we live on

No more rent-stabilized apartment buildings
with bags of overflowing garbage piled up out front

Just Victorian houses
with porches and ancient trees

pathways of layered song

Lines from Brooklyn Fortune Cookies

You will get good advice from your super's grandson's niece.

Stoop-sale your way to enlightenment, or at least two-dollar Danskos.

All museums resemble your best friend from kindergarten who taught you how to cross out your name.

That beard makes you look like Walt Whitman, but only if you whistle on the ferry at dusk.

If you give your subway seat to the pregnant woman in hooker heels, you should feel less guilty about taking the last teabag in the office lounge.

Eavesdrop with prowess and you will be rewarded in Facebook likes.

The state of God resides either inside the everything bagel hole or between the snowflake crystals that fell on your nose when you first kissed your future wife.

The mouse in the wall wishes you would buy organic.

You will discover that star anise is the most underused treasure in the spice cabinet.

Before the bus arrives, call your mother.

Before the apocalypse comes, make friends with the owner of the local diner.

Eat more grandma slices. Drink fewer papaya drinks.

You will read a book about the failure of democracy on a subway car surrounded by strangers who moved here from other countries and states.

Avoid mansplainers, manspreaders, man-haters, man buns, mandates and mayonnaise.

Don't name your dog Frank O'Hara if you've only read *Lunch Poems.*

You are a good explainer but a better echo.

The future is un...

You will fall in love with a woman in a hijab watching a YouTube video on how to braid hair.

That shade of black suits you.

Say goodbye to your local bakery, laundromat, hippie food café and shoe repair.

You should get a Ph.D. in complaining.

If you hadn't dropped out of Hebrew school, you might have married an Israeli.

Your insults sound better in French.

To become a great artist, become a better gossip.

By the time you finish eating this cookie, your block will be 37 percent more gentrified.

You will miss the Coney Island fireworks but enjoy the descriptions online.

A Short Essay on Middle Age

I'm always in airports, running down narrow passageways, but never on planes. I'm always in seafood restaurants but never eating fish. In my dreams, every European city looks like the Pacific Northwest. If I dream of Seattle, it's an exaggerated version: every road is a thin bridge, every cloud pierced by a mountain. If I dream of my parents, they're still living in my childhood home. (My dream-self sometimes breaks in to throw parties). If I dream of my husband, there's always the danger of him turning into a high school or college boyfriend, some smudge of a memory floating above the indoor arboretum. When the real husband reappears, his body flickering into focus as if viewed through glass underwater, it's not just him becoming more vivid—it's the whole room, the objects on the dream nightstand become shinier and more detailed, the curtains on the window turn suddenly from chainmail to mustard yellow silk.

Love Poem in a Failed State

Some mornings
when I am
just a typo
in pajamas
and the rain
is the thick
black eyeliner
around
an unseen sun,
the glimpse
of your left eye
opening under
the blankets
is enough
of a welcome
to flip the bird
to despair,
to allow myself
to feel each
one of my fingers
wiggling itself
awake.

The Cat We Don't Own

sleeps on my chest
and doesn't meow.
Instead it murmurs
in the voice of
my 81-year-old
mother, who is stuck
in a cardiac hospital
thousands of miles
away. Okay,
I admit it's not
my mom's actual
voice: the sound
the animal makes
is part growl, part purr,
part metallic laugh.
It's not really a cat
either. It's half cat,
half miniature rhino.
When I dream,
the chimera enters
my eyeholes and crawls
around, searching
for a subway car
with wings, so we
can fly together over
the veins of highways,
and splotchy landfills.
As my husband
turns away pulling
the blanket towards him,
I hold the not-cat
to my chest,
and I can hear
my mother's heart

under the animal's
thick black fur. It's
beating too fast,
too irregular, so
I know that it
wants to escape its
animal body,
wants to stomp its
feet in blood red
flamenco shoes,
wants to cry out,
to borrow the sun's
bullhorn, to scream
at anyone who'll listen.

THE HAPPINESS FACTORY

Abecedarian with Butchered Catalogue

America, I have given you nothing and now I am
butter, carved up to resemble a beauty queen at the Dubuque

county fair. Am I supposed to be nostalgic for the Technicolor era?
Dumbstruck by others' gee-whiz narratives, buck-toothed and over-

eager for honeysuckle cupcakes on the half shell? Believe it?
Forget it? Who cares if the past wears its dirty underwear to every

gala, hops the freight train even though it's going underground,
heaving with cash? You can smell its history seeping through, feel

its wet toes mucking up the inside of your boots or
jizzing up the dance floor, clogging the airwaves with KKK-brand

kazoos. Back up for a second! I am trying to find my brainmobile.
Look, we all want more than 51 dust bunnies in our pockets.

More than anything I miss my past life as an unkissed frog,
not for nothing was my teenagehood packaged in pretzel bits

or sold for scraps. Truth is, my dreamlife is overstuffed with
pancakes. I wake up each morning pressing the same button, so

quit laughing already. Stop holding your hand over your
right lung and looking cuter than me. America, admit you

stuffed the ballot box with freedom fries and crying-face emojis.
Tough lovage. Smart cookware. Try wearing this face paint

underwater, then tell me the best way to cry. I don't need another
victory to know the wind-up top is rigged. How many more broken

windows until we realize our house *is* the wind, even the air is
X-rated, hidden under police tape. Where were you when this particular

yelling started? I was here with a broken camera, waiting for a future to
zoom into or out of, to clarify, to somehow unmake sense.

We Were on the Way to the Protest March or Brunch

When I say
my tweet
is a bullet
headed
straight
into the heart
of Capitalism,
who is wearing
a frayed
Cookie Monster
costume
stolen from
a West Texas
frat house,
what I mean is
that words
are the net
that keeps
the acrobats
from falling
into the gaping
mouths of
the uncontrollable
masses,
and this
is why,
when I
think
there is
a possibility
for instant
change,

the color of
my sunset Bellini
looks more
sunrise,
less sunset—
the café's
white
painting is
suddenly
more Mallarmé,
less *Architectural Digest,*
1986.

Benediction for a New Year

I said I am letting my anger disappear

I said I am letting my anger become the word anger

I said my anger is not a puckered mouth

I said anger is so 2017

I said if you are going to disturb my nap

why not do it with sunlight giraffing
the window ajar?

I said let my shackles be bedazzled

fake jade-encrusted   scented
with knitted begonias

I said why not just let the plastic
fuchsia flamingos release

their primal molting into the future

I said let this ass-breaking
chipmunked-cheeked afternoon end

like the clang of an Xmas ax

I said that sometimes bad news
tastes like good whiskey

I said we might as well lie down
I said we might as well be laid

down on the highway

I said we might as well stay down
in the highway

and pretend history   is the truck
running us over

I said I forgot what

I said I was trying to   I said I had

I said I meant I   I said I

I said if you want to know what it feels like

to be a woman
these days   just swallow

some uncomfortable shoes

Muriel Said That to Be a Jew in the 20th Century Is to Be Offered a Gift

> "Late Friday night, several hundred torch-bearing men and women marched on the main quadrangle of the University of Virginia's grounds, shouting, 'You will not replace us,' and 'Jews will not replace us.'"
>
> —*The New York Times, August 11, 2017*

We New York City kids always felt superior,
but then I wake up and it's 2017, and suddenly
I'm all jealous of the cold rocks under other
people's feet: the kids who got the coolest bullies
to sign their leg casts are now CEOs rewriting
the meaning of cloud script. *Resist, fail, and resist.*
Mrs. Whitebread's been in the same hallway
for thirty years pretending we didn't see her
crying behind the history textbook, triggered
by the passage her family erased. So why
not just fold your childhood into a terrycloth
swan? Ignore the blobs of bubble wrap, dirty
erasers—the mountains of cell batteries
in a place whose name you can't pronounce.

*

In a place whose name you can't—
you try to embrace the rage, *the stone insanity*
with all its cracks. Run into the crowded street,
the Bill of Rights written on your ass in eyeliner,
so the enemies you moon will finally understand
the uses of free speech. Click, pause, reset.
Become the anger you envy in other people.
Ignore the paperwork, bills, piles of laundry.
What color is the parachute of an airplane
in flames? Your future career was meant to be
an asteroid or telepathic frog. What happened?
Your new password is FUCKTHAT. Your
username is: theMemoryofSlaveryRacismLoss.

*

The memory of slavery, racism, loss
is not the same as the feeling of remembering
slavery, racism, loss. What you thought
was the ghost of the 20th century is just
a mustard-yellow bikini top tied to
a sunburnt toddler at the public pool
in Park Slope, Evanston or Marin.
So little is covered, so why is it still around?
And who are we to complain? Former children
to the accidents of privilege. Born to families
with two-car garages, glass-door bookcases
and folk-song-packed grade-school assemblies
where white children sing songs about Rosa Parks.
Is this what we thought democracy looked like?

*

This is what we thought democracy
looked like: reading poetry in the sandbox,
the ocean removing its rubber mask,
revealing tongue-shaped retractable blades.
The kids' books we read on our parents'
faux-Chinese sofas included details
about charred bodies and lamps made
from human skin. Dear Reader, fill in
the details of your own tragedy. History,
please explain—how does comfort end
and responsibility begin? Privilege,
when will you flip over, and let us listen
to the B-side, the one where if you play it
backwards, the present moment makes sense?

*

Backwards, does the present moment make sense?

At 18, I fell in love with an activist, and we spent our days in the Texas heat, walking around parking lots with clipboards gathering signatures for water regulation. I never completely believed in the reality of the world, felt more myself in the dissolving boundaries of de Kooning's blurry yellow. Even with clipboard in hand, did I have faith in my own relationship to the Earth? I couldn't feel it.

I didn't need to. I rented other people's passion.

One evening, I borrowed a housemate's vase so my boyfriend could display the algae from the polluted lake to the city council. A fancy vase was all she had, opaque, orange glass with spiderlike designs. I think it was from Pottery Barn.

Of course, he lost the prop in the chaos of the hearing. My housemate was furious.

I was working on an essay on dolls in Rilke and Djuna Barnes that night, far from downtown, so I couldn't tell her where it had ended up.

In the next day's *Statesman,* the story ended with a joke about the abandoned vase. No one could tell the reporter why that vessel was sitting on the floor.

*

No
one
could
tell
the
reporter

why
that
vessel
was
sitting
on
the
floor

*

Why was that vessel sitting on the floor?
Are we the vase, the water or the algae?
The clouds and the towers are not enough
to hide the country we maybe always were
or are. *Here in this divided time.* Here
with these conflicting signs. I watch the news
in a small-town hotel room on the way
to visit my husband's Trump-voting dad.
On my laptop, a blurry photo of a young
woman holding up a handwritten sign:
THIS IS THE MOMENT HEBREW SCHOOL
PREPARED ME FOR, and I think of
Rukeyser's words, *The gift is torment,*
but also *full life.*

Notes:

In "Muriel Said That to Be a Jew in the 20th Century Is to Be Offered a Gift," the lines in italics are from Muriel Rukeyser.

Household Tips for a New Era

Protect the Constitution using a musical instrument carved from an abandoned sofa.

Bake a cake shaped like the world you want to become.

Instead of a stripper, put your loud-mouthed uncle and his cable TV inside.

Frost the cake with Coca-Cola buttercream, so he has no desire to leave.

Imagine your lungs belong to a 10-foot dolphin.

Remember to breathe for more than one person.

Test the air for the spit molecules of self-proclaimed patriots.

With the right *je ne sais quoi*, a non-stick muffin pan might double as a rape defense mechanism.

Wear the right shade of half-price eye shadow to see clearly under martial law.

Write down what you see, laminate and label.

Invent a new language out of the sounds the vacuum cleaner makes when it's unplugged.

Hand-wash your ideals.

Believe in fragments, cloud language, glass doorknobs and quarter tones.

Sweep away stereotypes, candy wrappers, canned sitcom laugher
and empty Viagra bottles.

Knit a blanket large enough to cover the history of denial.

Hide your magnified solidarity under lavender potpourri.

Sing to the baby in your sling.

Translate the pedagogy of her cries.

To a New Era

(February 2017)

Fuck you with your tufts of violence
growing above your groin,
with your busted lip called media
and your automatic, imitation-
platinum blade-studded cock ring
circling a planet you're ready to destroy.

The old era may have been a fragment
floating in an ocean of private prisons,
chicken-shit rivers, and remote-
controlled wars, but it smelled like lilacs
and artistically sourced lattes
and it knew how to read at a 12th-grade level.

Unlike you, who reduces Wollstonecraft's
Vindication of the Rights of Women
to a garbled idiom tattooed in micro-script
above Frankenstein's monster's blazing pee-hole.

Please, gods of sunlight and morning naps,
goddesses of semicolons, give us
another chance to welcome in
the better angels of nurture,

to open our arms wide enough that our flesh
becomes a stained-glass house
the exile can find comfort in and recreate
out of whispers and tulip hearts.

Let our desire for kindness be larger
than the sickness of our fear.

Search Engine Overlord

The dystopian surface
with the one-thousand-percent cotton
lining is not enough to satiate
the present, or unmake
the water buffalo
of the past.   No thumbs
needed to call off
an impractical joke.
No roof parade. No
uncomfortable topiary
helmet to ruin your
dismissive eyebrow slant.
Frenemy happy hour
for all. (Yum!)
            Freedom zucchini fries
on the half shell. *Yes* to the toe jam.
Maybe to the hot-sauce prayer-
closet electioneering headache
medicine plus one. I'm trying
to be more perfect, but instead
I'm in-between and frog-ready,
Mama-proof post-industrial
complex. *Play that fruitful music*
lost girl et al. Some days
all of my favorite plotlines end
with a woman walking *into*
a roof. Freedom for all, even
you, squeaking your way back
into the corset narrative you
thought had been transformed.
Nope! Just signposts here:
the activist who lights himself
on fire becomes a favorite

art-house icon and then a parody
on the Simpsons only .0003
percent of the audience
"gets." Our fingers hurt
from dialing other people's
senators. Wake up, canary face!
Time for your solo.

President's Day

Before George, there was another
first president,

his flesh carved
from the body
of a cherry tree,
veins full of
pre-linguistic vowels,   primordial auburn sludge.

They say it was he

who divided the states   into genders:

the South, a buoyant mouse-
hearted femme fatale,
the North,

male as an oak, or the word "oak"
in the crease of a dusty forestry textbook.

I am telling a lie.

The first president's face couldn't bear fruit.
Instead of lips, there was a branding iron.

When he kissed,   he burned
his partner's lips (my lips?),   so they

looked like   *his* lips.

Not too ugly, but when I sucked on them
they tasted   like hate.

When the rivers voted for him,
the earth cratered in shame.

We made love in the mud,
but it wasn't love, and his brain

seeped into my brain until I became
the president and he became the slave,

became the wife, the broken broom
and the cracking sky.

I felt the power of that,
but wanted more than power,

so I said,
"let's start over," but

the fires had already started
and there was water

in my iron shoes
and in the glass archive

I thought was his (or my)
brain and in my agate-

lightning-full eyes, so all
that was left of our romance

was the skin that created it,
was the sound of the paper skin,

creasing and ripping when the other
first president's axe finally hit.

A Short Essay on Protest

In fourth grade, I refused to go to school until the principal met with me about the teacher who I said was cruel. In his office, Dr. Swan agreed, the teacher was a bully but also old. I should take pity on her outdated ways. As he handed me a mint lollipop, I watched his turtles circling each other in the terrarium.

I wonder if I have overlearned this lesson. I have a tendency to imagine what each murderous policeman was like at age five, punched in the nose for having the audacity to cry. I picture our racist president as a baby, dropped on the ground so many times that the fire of earth, as an act of mercy, swallowed him and replaced him with his gangrenous double. At night, I dream about their kinder shadows. I envision their blurrier selves waking up at 3 a.m. sitting in empty living rooms in the dark, drinking lumpy, microwaved hot chocolate.

This afternoon, when another black teenager was shot, my anger became a yelping beast trapped in a cage by my pity. I felt disgusted by my pity, knew my anger was righteous but was unable to let it out. I wondered *What good is an angry dog when what is needed is …*

As I turn the radio off, I imagine the nation I was taught we were—try to unlearn the myth I memorized for the test. I destroy the fence built of misplaced compassion, I take the pieces and turn them into shields.

I attempt to make a clearing for my anger. I watch it digging up the bones that rot beneath the field. I imagine it tangled in the muddy roots, paddling in the polluted underground river, its howl transfiguring the dark water into fire.

I still know nothing about successful protest.

In the Spleen of the City

The bad witness and the activist meet for coffee at the center of the city.

She is wearing a dress the color of a liar's tears. He is wearing a frog mask that resembles a dirty ghost.

They chat about their childhoods in opposite-coast suburbias. In both towns, their bedrooms smelled like paperbacks and imitation vanilla.

They each had a friend who used to prick herself with beaded safety pins. Different young girls. Different colored pins.

Who is the activist? Who is the bad witness? Neither can remember.

If they kiss, their tongues will split into lightning forks and broken flutes.

*

When the bad witness was an activist, she used to chain herself to her sister—or was it a doll?

She often forgets that she never had a sister.

At the playground, she would go up to babies and yell, "You're not my sister."

As an activist, she believes in the reality of the world.

*

The bad witness gets a job as a poet-in-residence at a tattoo parlor, but all of her poems are just one word, *stop*. It's an improvement on her pre-amnesia poems, and small enough to fit on most bodies without unbearable pain.

*

Across town, classrooms are being used to stockpile invisible guns.

The frogs who sleep in the desks clamor for air, while the android teacher thinks her memory of her past life as a science-fiction action star is only a dream.

*

Years pass, and the coffee shop starts serving moonshine right into people's mouths. No cup needed. It's the only way to deal with the constant lying.

As the activist and the bad witness chat, one of their bodies is replaced with a metal cage.

Now he (or she?) is only an iron structure, an enclosure of air with a dumb whale heart, beating inside.

Neither notices the missing flesh—the almost empty construction where a chest used to be.

Not True/False but Quality-Controlled Red-State Picaresque

In my headphones, voices:

Farewell sonic glimpses   *Hello ghost telephones*

In the briefing room,
the reporter's laugh—

the planet of D.C.   shining bulbous

another clown nose threatening to replace

the terrestrial with a whirlpool
of cosmic slop

No clouds   to obstruct the view
of strangers exchanging

face sandwiches

Just another 4th wave
ism for us

a knock-knock   macaroni necklace

to hang some troubles here

Margaret Thatcher Dies the Same Day Neruda's Bones Are Exhumed

The ocean is made of future ghosts.

A new ante-mood-essence bumps
against time and into an atmosphere

which has been waiting for a bicycle
it calls justice to open

the way through the cranium
hemisphere and into the sky.

The leaves today all sing
through ash.

A green voice scratches
the light switch in the sparrow's brain.

The secrets of the dead hide
in the fingernails of the living.

What good is good?

We Are Being Delayed by Super Vision

We thought seeing *into*
could be a substitute for seeing past

No lies   No trainwreck histrionics

Sometimes you go so far
into an impulse

you come out the other side
as unalloyed broken-knife rage

You say

We are being delayed
by the possibility of change

And we laugh,

not because it isn't true
but because

why the hell not

There's nutmeg singing jingles in the aisles

There's an ad for word-processing software
featuring meatballs and sulfured wings

You want to believe me now
You want to replace me now

A man smashes his cardboard sign
on his helmet,

once again mistakes a beautiful etcetera
for a righteous plan

Justin Bieber Visits the Anne Frank House

A young girl in neon orange is not an iced donut,
despite a shared resemblance to sprinkles.

Light bounces off the elevated expressway's
passing cars.

Here is a white apple.
There is a whiter sun.

A rattling bicycle doesn't need
words to be understood.

On the curb, a pink suitcase,
almost bursting, stuffed with loss.

My heart is a door,
the color of cracked walnuts,

says the woman
on the stoop.

What color is that?
asks the air.

Ode to Unhappiness

"Ordinary unhappiness is a long poem"
—David Shapiro

Thank you, ordinary unhappiness, for the beep
of the smoke alarm when the battery dies,

the cloud of spoiled milk ruining beautiful
bitter coffee. Thank you for the ash-colored grout

that will never get clean, for the smell of garbage
we are too tired to haul down the stairs. Thank you

for the luxury of that sliver of luck—the ability
to turn off the cell and the television, to recycle

the newspaper with the headline about toddlers
in cages. Thank you for the fluke of the far away,

for the dream about clear wild deer walking
through closed city windows. Thank you

for late afternoon boredom, for ripped leggings
and unaired sitcom pilots, for songs too remote

to be required to hear. Thank you for the rustle
of swinging car parts and inside-out violins,

and for the warmth of your orange catlike
body, snuggling quietly between us,

the ghost mouse of a future, weirder sadness,
wriggling slowly in your closed jaw.

The World Is Burning, but Everyone Needs Sleep

Why bother to lift the cloud's galvanic veil?
Why remove the halo contact lenses
from my solid white eyes?

If so many crows like to watch the blurred
screen of my face, how can I be expected
to understand the truth of the obstinate
fire hydrant? The meaning of the space
between the prongs of the unplugged iron?

Maybe it's enough to bask in the shadows
of the thighs of the monumental icon,
to rescue dented souls with the tongs
of a sparkling imagination, to stretch out

on the floor of our carpeted basement,
counting the heads of our ceramic turtle collection
until the meditative gesture
becomes you, and you it.

So don't ask me to sleep on the other side
of the bottled-water bed.

Don't tell me to flick on the light and stop
drinking cocoa from the Van Gogh
museum's ear-shaped mug.

Yes, there may be a river of tomato-juice blood
surrounding our neoclassical-pueblo duplex condo,
but that doesn't mean the blinds should be open,
and everything allowed in.

Who Else Should I Not Trust with Language?

(For Paula Cisewski)

While the dolphins were fermenting social metamorphoses, mite-sized gods hijacked the agenda.

Now all anyone wants to talk about is what Angelina Jolie's teeth look like from outer space. (Answer: abandoned drive-in movie screens.)

It's not your fault if this makes you want to sob into your Disney-trademarked Mickeyccino.

Everyone feels that.

Sometimes I'll be posting my status update and all I can see is the expanding space between the letters.

The beautiful sad whiteness of it like a mountain-sized scoop of vanilla ice cream sculpted by Jean Arp in 1948.

It's like that substance in the two-day-old soaking pan of what used to hold lasagna—after a while the grayness forms a language of its own.

Broken Singularity, Kali Tribe Sestina

—For Mary Beth Edelson

We fought for clear doors and portable arias.
Our cities magnified invisible faces, broadcast
our smiles on oversized television billboards.
Our children wrote transformative placards
in the womb, burst forth with their left hands
already in raised fists, preparing for travel.

Did we envy our babies, imagining their travels,
how they'd leave history behind them like arias
shattering the space-time continuum, hand in hand,
grabbing armfuls of flaming whatevers, broadcasting
radical change like a spell? Maybe. But placards,
not poetry, taunted us. The city's billboards

formed a cage around our hope. Too many billboards.
Not enough reinvention of post-capitalist travel.
Where was the ideology that could transcend the placard,
could transform jingles into ricocheting, opalescent arias?
We called it "hope" (i.e. the soul's internal broadcast)
and tried to manifest it by grabbing the future's hands.

Did we believe everything the world tried to hand
us was potentially malleable—that a flashing billboard
could be transformed into a true haiku, and not a broadcast
advertisement for designer seaweed? Did we think travel
was enough to change the sound of a bullet to an aria?
We tried to convince ourselves the blank and spiritual placard

we held above the burning city was more than a placard.
We hoped its blankness could change minds; hand
us a way of unboxed being. Some days, listening to arias
streaming from my computer's speakers, billboards

blurred by sunlight and the shadows of passing travels,
I'd watch it slip between the cracks in the pending broadcast.

In these moments, I could hear the music beneath the broadcast
and watch its notes wrap themselves in wet leaves, soft placards
encircling pain. I'd slip wishes inside the slim volumes of travels.
I wanted to believe in this, in nothing else. I wanted to hand
over my future in the present tense, to ignore the billboards
for war and shopping, but I knew I needed more than an aria's

reprieve from suffering. No song would be enough to broadcast
the reverberating empathy required to upend the billboard and the
placard.
No open hand would be open enough. There is no travel but travel.

History Lesson

With the invention of photography,
pupils started to shrink. Babies were
born with lit pinpricks instead of eyes.

This led women to think of their unclothed
bodies as *naked* instead of *nude*, to darken
their nipples with black whispers and wax.

This led men to calculate the speed
of the first great avalanche, to measure
the distance between mountain and lung.

When images digitized, fingerprints
blurred. Women noticed that their tears
had the potential to be sexy if they wore

them inside out so the dry interior
hid the messy wetness of the drop's
skin. Blood too transformed into

an idea about loss or pedigree.
Veins filled with periwinkle regret,
pixel dust and newspaper confetti.

Lovers could feel their palms drying up,
coconut trees replacing the eggs
their fingers used to hatch.

Boredom

is a skinny green
tree who tries
to gain weight
by eating rainbow
sprinkle dingdongs
and playing
cellphone Tetris.
How long will
it take for
the universe
to decipher
the meaning of
his yawn?
If you weighed it,
it would levitate,
would rejigger
the sadness
hidden in each
shifting pause,
but he, he
can't feel
his own leaves
through his
borrowed
snow mittens,
and he doesn't
know how
to recreate
the feeling
of being born.
All he wants
to do is to
repost his

frenemy's
status updates
on his ugliest bark,
shake a little
confetti entitlement
on the trail,
trade on his
good looks
for hot
leafy cash.

The Adjunct Commuter

I'm waiting for the bus and imagine the street is made
of money, but it's not the type of money accepted on this
planet or any planet. Sometimes I'm waiting for the bus
and I see the word "new" projected on people's faces, but
not my own. I am no longer new. What are you if you
aren't new? The bus is on the left side, and I am on the right.
I am waiting for the bus, but I am only wearing my Underoos,
and my stuffed cat can't get on the bus because she doesn't
have a MetroCard, and I am trying to pay the fare with a wallet
full of pigeon blood. It multiplies as it spills through the center
of the empty bus, foaming mouths at the edges of bloody waves.
My clones wear animal masks (lion, flamingo, toad) while we wait
for the bus. The bus is inside my skin riding my spine. None of us
is small enough to get inside it. I don't care where the bus
is going anymore, but I want to be on it. Have you ever kissed
an august Buddha in the marsupial pouch of a bus? It feels
like being the soul of oatmeal, but better. Everyone I have
ever loved is on that bus. They are going to a protest, but nobody
remembers what the issue is, or the issue keeps changing,
like the words on the signs: the name of the candidate
or the name of the war. We are going to the march because
we want to be together, but aren't. We are waiting for different
buses that don't arrive. Waiting for a bus from inside an iceberg,
and before we can get on the bus, the icebergs have to melt.
We want them to melt because we haven't had sex in twenty-four
and a half days, or because we like to eat grass-fed lamb burgers
in the back of a rhinestone stretch limousine that circles Alaska
before we can even find the bus stop. It's possible I fell asleep
and we are all melting icebergs waiting for the bus, flooding
Foster Avenue with salt water and half-frozen chunks of displaced
whale spirits. One day I am waiting so long for the bus that I forget
I am waiting for a bus and find myself inventing music, dairy-free
béchamel and urban tetherball. They crown me the biggest shark
in the biggest city of the universe, and I am on every TV channel,

big-toothed, grinning like I'm the host or something, but nobody
 watches
TV anymore. Everyone would rather be writing post-linguistic poetry
or studying artisanal adzuki bean canning. If a woman smiles on TV
and nobody watches yadda yadda, you know. So I go back to my
 bus stop,
remember I should have been waiting for the bus. I enjoy waiting
for buses. I'm a bus waiter. There's beauty in waiting for the bus.

Self-Portraits in Late Capitalism

1. He took his blood pressure and recorded the number for the day. Then wrote a poem with that exact number of words in it, diluting every verb with a solution of Diet Coke and sulfuric acid.

2. She weighed herself on the drugstore scale. Bought a package of chewing gum, skin-clearing concealer or tomato soup for every pound over the ideal number. Made a totem pole of the objects with a printed Instagram of her best duck face positioned on top.

3. They added the value of their bank account and the value of their assets. Shrunk this number to the size of a pinprick and used these quasi-pixels to create an image of their favorite reproduction mid-century sofa.

4. I added the number of my Facebook friends and Twitter followers. Subtracted the number of people (and/or businesses or nonprofits or imaginary/dead figures) who did not follow me back. Added the number of followers who I did not follow back. Hired a factory in Shenzhen to produce neon copies of this number to light the closet, which real estate brokers call "my Brooklyn apartment."

5. We recalculated our SAT scores for today's measurements and baked the numbers into a tangerine-colored pot lollipop, which we both licked while sitting on the rusted fire escape while first-graders dressed in red and orange post-digital wings pretended to storm the poem.

The Happiness Factory

No one gets rich teaching students to build pigeon-
shaped dwellings, but it's not a bad way to ignore
the mountain crumbling to the east, or to pretend
you don't notice the smell of smoke drifting in

from the north. I know some of my students
would rather be asleep in bed, and that others are
daydreaming about pre-gaming with their ancestors.
They have a faraway look in their eyes as if their

great-grandmother is holding their ponytail up
during a quick before-party hurl. Some students
are so present that I can feel their cheeks vibrating
away from their skulls. Once a student touched

my ankle when I was half-asleep. I kindly explained
I was happily married, but I was so flattered
that the rest of the day everything I ate
tasted like chocolate-hazelnut Kahlúa gelato.

Inside some pigeons, chrysanthemums blossom.
Within others, blue monsters made out of frozen
vodka open their mouths to the dark. Some pigeons
have bright yellow wheels that flash like traffic lights.

Others hide their mobility under unflappable wings.
One day students threw chairs across the room.
I hid beside an industrial stapler near a half-built bird.
When the commotion ended, the room smelled like salt

and moist armpits. Some students asked *Why are we*
building the birds? Will people actually use them
as their homes or will they be primarily for travel?
How will they be distributed? How much will they cost?

I made up stories depending on who was in the room.
I'd tell them that one pigeon was being built to shelter
a future god. Another would be used to store a special
refrigerator capable of reproducing the food removed

from its shelves. I told them of "top secret" designs.
One would be so comfortable that its silk pillows
would instantly cure PTSD, and another would be
so quick it would travel faster than a rumor on Twitter.

I often said that if we became experts at building
the birds it wouldn't even matter if our planet
died. The pigeons could be our new homes.
It wouldn't matter that none of us had a key.

I HAVE A SECRET CRUSH ON EVERYONE IN THE WORLD

Listen to the Rooster

The two-headed hermaphrodite
    pig-of-the-sky will one day
split into a man and into a woman,
    but I will still be a rooster,
and my beak will still ache when the wind
    blows through it, and my crown
will still rattle when the wind becomes it.

Last night I pecked at the earth,
    but no seed sprouted from it.
Last night I pecked at the earth, but no
    seed sprouted from it.

The ground was still red as the sky.
    The sky was still red as my feathery crown.
One day the Earth will split into planets:
    a planet of knowledge and a planet of sleep.
One day the Earth will spin into multiple selves,
    and the woman and the man will be
multiple too, splitting themselves into ears and shoulders,
    into music and bones, into a circus of miniature
multiplying hermaphrodite pigs-of-the sky—

    so many hermaphrodite pigs-of-the-sky
that the pigs will be stars in themselves, a spiraling
    galaxy of hermaphrodite flickering pigs
who will one day each split into women and men,
    into bodies and starlight, into beak dust
and astral blossoms, into a gazillion microscopic
    pigs-of-the-sky, made of red earth, red sky
and fire, made from the threads of my rooster song,
    from the yelp and the yowl, from the hush
and the wail, and from the oblong gap in the shape
    of my rust-gilded squawk.

Old Weather

We are waiting for something to help screw
the sky's head back, so we don't acknowledge

the luminous Unsaid, that black coat slipping
off the damp back of our missing father.

One can only pretend to have patience for
so long before the roof falls into the childhood

basement and a mountain of avocado shag carpet
envelops memories of half-consummated sex.

The steeple, like any other work of beauty,
pretends to pray for the end of thinking.

The bull, like any other bovine, pretends to offer us
fresh milk, baring its tiny nipples to the sky.

If the dead father were here, he would tell us to stop
making a fuss. Poor man, he was always trying

to say something about the nature of mankind,
but what we actually wanted from him was to let

the sun unfasten its nose, to allow the scent of ripe
blueberries to change the color of the light bulb.

He told us that one way to convince yourself that
you're human is to cry, but a better way is to hold

yourself completely still, so that the heart of the forest
enters your bloodstream, replaces your cells with fresh

crunchy fronds. Only then will you no longer be bothered
by the pale silver screams reverberating from the city's

canned juice plant. Only then will you feel like an actual
part of the world, something more real than just leafy ideas.

Lavender

"Being in a funk" is what the cool people call it.

It's the purple that surrounds the scene at the lake.
Not sad enough to actually drown.

You say, "I'm in a funk," and I think you think
you're too pretty, too well groomed,
too stylishly disheveled, to actually sulk.

Have you ever tried drinking a milkshake
with a girlfriend in a funk?

She just stares at the straw as if sucking on it
would allow the whole world into her mouth.

When a teenager wears baggy sweatpants
all February, her math teacher may ask her
if she's in a funk.

(She's actually just pissed off.)

Frogs don't get into funks, but toads do.

In the Bible, Abraham thought Sarah was in a funk,
but she was actually shaking with grief.

When her baby arrived, her 100-year-old flesh
quivered like a sliced papaya.

There is nothing funky
about being in a funk.

The Polish biochemist Casimir Funk
invented vitamins.

The golfer Fred Funk wore a pink skirt
to settle a bet with Annika Sörenstam.

Doing cartwheels or changing the bed sheets
are suggested cures for getting out of a funk.

To be in a funk is to want to cry,
but to be unable to access tears.

To be in a funk is to be unable to hear
the music in the subway's rattle.

If Virginia Woolf had been in a funk,
she would have filled her pockets
with dead lilacs instead of rocks.

The Poetry Reading

The mustached cowboy-hatted thrice-divorced
old-man poet famous for sleeping with flaxen-haired
(or was it flax-seed eating?) quote-unquote
nubile graduate students is at the podium
reading his poem personifying a wedding dress—
how sad it is, all alone in a dusty closet, how
it longs to be laid on a funeral pyre or set ablaze
next to the replica of Plath and Hughes' robin's-
egg-blue Terra Cruiser gas range, or was it
the neglected moonlit member of the old man
poet "breaking into blossom" or recoiling
from the memory of time passing faster than
the dust can settle on his brand-new Honda
Civic LX or ranch-style remodeled sunroom?
The audience is trying to remember what
ingredients they need to pick up for tomorrow's
paella, what that email said about the time
of that meeting with Suzanne about assessment.
They are alternately trying to remember
if they remembered to order that Minecraft book
for a nephew's 8th birthday party and worrying
if their Facebook-level "friends" notice that
their purple cat socks clash with their scuffed
burgundy clogs, and at a certain point, the poem
has gone on for so long no one can tell if
the old-man poet is still personifying that
wedding dress or if a headless wedding dress
has taken his place at the podium. We look up
from the cell phones we are hiding in our laps,
and there it stands—smoky and lacy
in front of the glowing microphone
in the corner of the basement bookstore,
104 miles from the nearest artist colony,
the flaming dress is burning like a 12-hour

candle, or like the lost poetry of an elderly
Rimbaud written on the slats of sunken ships,
and the dress itself has grown a mouth,
and in the middle of its flames its lips
belt out a new poem, about fake
cowboy poets, how sad they are, how alone.

History Lesson

The sister ship to the Titanic was the Gigantic.
She was supposed to be the prodigal daughter,
the boat with the good personality
people said was too wide to marry.

She disappeared before
she had a chance to return.

While her sister filled with elegant crowds
in lace cravats and ivory rolled spats,
she sat in the harbor stuffing her portholes
with meat lover's pizza.

They used to say that if the Titanic were
a gin & tonic, the Gigantic would be
a salty pint glass michelada.

She floated through history backwards,
a ghost liner draped in algae
and bone-filled fishing nets.

She disappeared before
she had a chance to return.

This Tyger Burns the Bones of William Blake (Or, Self-Portrait as Poem)

The body of the text
resembles me
before plastic surgery.

The idea of the text
resembles me
after.

Death isn't
plural,
just two-faced.

If you want to become
the red dress
of poetry,

you need to wear
control-top
pantyhose.

Without those
terminal
constraints

language
would be
liquid wasp:

a head devoured
by milky synapses
and need.

Kerosene

(after Frank O'Hara)

Ah drone butterflies
when you think of them
dropping polished
"like" buttons
in hologram stork mouths
you know how wonderful
the 21st century
can be
and the gilded teeth marks
on the monitors
invisible and historic buzzes
clothed in data
slightly Jello-y
like a Mike Kelley

there is the mystery of loss
somewhere inside
our fingers pause
we invented this era
with our flying
which is blue and pillowy

we owe a debt to
our wires and to Mark Zuckerberg
for playing Scrabble
in our lungs
before we were born

we don't do much ourselves
but click and chew
write emails
to our kinder

doppelgängers
who are waiting
for the retweets to arrive
and who else cries
it is our habit
to obscure

how are you living
in broken December
I am angry like a cupcake
in an éclair factory

how dare you
you were
made in the shape
of our demographic
I was not
I was made between
the wings of a drone canary
"with a surgical strike carved
from nostalgia"
except for fear (just listen)
I am in love with this century
for being so complicated
but still I have to weep

Notes:

"Kerosene" is a line-by-line "rewriting" of Frank O'Hara's poem "Naphtha."

Semifreddo

Despite a Ph.D. in culinary architecture, no one ate my cakes. I told this to my mother, who thought I was making a double entendre, but I was 47, past the age when one revels in dirty jokes.

To be a failure in a city of failures would be one thing, but I was a citizen of Rocket City, USA, where every day boys in skin-colored bathing suits jump from needle-shaped buildings, and teach themselves to glide midair.

I had wanted to build structures confident in their impermanence: cathedrals made of smells where you'd be able to recall what it felt like to crawl for the first time, or classrooms where children could lick their desks and spend the rest of their time making vermillion pudding creatures on sunlit, slippery mats.

Instead, each day I woke to the sound of a monstrous bell. Without noticing, I had become the bell myself.

Crunch!

After eating the last piece
of the last potato chip,
Happiness tries on his
wife's lavender nightgown,
swallows an ice cube and hides
his ego in the cookie jar
with his rage. Souls seep
from the photographs
that stole them and back
into the bodies where they
were born. After eating
the last crumb of the last
potato chip, the world feels
smaller. Ghosts curl under
pillows, fantasize about
the invention of a belt that
won't fall off. Puffy shadows
trace their edges with Q-tips
damp from tears. After licking
the last piece of salt off
the last potato chip, eyes
butter themselves: smear
vision across time. No more
sunlight on my suntan.
No more wide-mouthed rain.

Hexagon

Susan thought Bobby would fall in love with her
when she wore her tutu decorated with toy tarantulas,
but Bobby was busy sewing a ball gown, the color of music,
hoping that when he wore it Billy would love him.
Billy wore a cape with boxing gloves attached, but
they were too small for his bulbous palms—and he
wasn't sure who he wanted to punch. Liza said she
wanted to be punched. She was wearing a nightgown
that made her look like a melting snowman and
blue leggings printed with blood-colored stars.
But who did the fabric love? What about the thread
encircling her pudgy thighs? What color shadow
did her left elbow secretly desire? Who would her
buttons twist for? What shape could dampen those lips?

Listen to What You Cannot Hear

At six a.m., the planet craters inward
like a teenage girl, half-afraid
of a full-length mirror, and the trees
stop shaking for a millisecond,
the clams and mussels open
their shells to the passing clouds
as if to say *hi, how are you* and mean it.

Is this why the security guards
at the museum hide themselves under
the sculptures so it's difficult to tell
what's art and what's human,
what's cow-spotted mountain and
what's mountain-spotted cow?
Perhaps this is why all the babies
are throwing their mashed-up carrots
in the air, why the social worker claims
she'd rather be a pre-sliced mango than a flag.

Still Life with Island

A crocodile sleeps
on the chest of a naked
sleeping woman.
The woman, like all
naked sleeping women,
is dreaming of
an alligator, and
the crocodile, like
all crocodiles,
is jealous of
the dream beast.

The sun, watching
from the gold
picture frame,
steps out
of the painting,
says,
            please forgive
the alligator
its glamour.
There's a sadness
that comes from slipping
beneath surfaces unseen,
from sleeping between
the cracks of
ambient rocks.

And so the weather
peels off her off-
white gloves, and
the clouds twist
in the sky like ripped
fishing nets.

And the crocodile,
like all crocodiles,
listens to what
the sun says,
tries to believe
what he hears.

Moveable Us

A pond relaxes into an art movement.
It pushes landward like a couch.

The indecent, clipped moons
inside the static multiply, stitched

together with lounge chairs and rebel
orthodontics, inhabited by another's films,

by a language with pressure, staggeringly
avid square birds and sentient doubts.

*

A woman tries radiating dog-eared
quietude. Half-mooned and moody.

She thinks "breakfast," but the world
hears "steak." She thinks it's time to tie

the ribbons on the invisible revolution,
but the world hears "party time,"

thinks "breasts." What starts as
a "window" ends up as a hole.

*

Instead of your mortal coffee, try to feel
the upright sidekick's psychic glimpsing.

Pour out the "meaning" in the "meaning vessels"
and press "go." Feel the change in atmospheric

pressure on your nose ring. Tabulate
the weight of your foster pit bull's shadow

with the power of your lungs. Revel
in the moment between, the arched pause.

*

A man and a woman each create a sculpture
of a question mark for the park. They follow

the same model, use the same materials.
The man's sculpture is described as an abstract

meditation on the nature of looking. The woman's
is a political statement about the nature of seeing.

No one is exactly wrong. Or particularly
right. All art is context. All context is a lie.

*

Sailboats don't need to sail to be beautiful.
A waitress probably shouldn't wait for a diner

to turn off the light, nor should a patient
be patient if she wants to survive

the ER room, but to dovetail from this—
You look down from your dusty book

and out the window. It's October.
Bus tires bloom with lilies of smoke.

*

Sometimes we wake up in one city
with a different city flowing in our veins.

On these days language is a gold-plated
or mud-crusted hinge on the box of the world.

One moment, you are thinking of kissing
the person you love, the next he's you—

and the sidewalks are bursting with onyx tulips,
charred wicks, wobbling tree-shaped love.

Listen to What I Am Saying, Not What I Say

Try to fold your memories as if you were handling
your mother's underwear

or as if the memories were the creases
in her face, your face.

Look at your destiny. It's over
there, the pink dress

pedaling the tricycle—a spirit
on wheels, doing a religious wheelie

like all the other false gods who
haunt your pungent suburb.

If you are sleeping, where is
your necklace of drool?

If you are awake, why does your headache
keep sticking its tongue on the frozen pole?

If anyone is a fan of the way the past
twists its tendrils around all the knobs,

let *her* be the first to throw our
hosiery over the glass wall.

How long can you hold on to
a mummified cat

when the building is
already burning?

Sometimes I just want to use
my own hands.

Mauve Decade

(for Guy Maddin)

Much has been made of our father's missing
memories. The captain discovered them,
book-fishing with his sister on a ship
made from black gills and rusted bones.

Memories? The captain discovered them
with his crush on a river of lost ships
made from black gills and rusted bones.
He was hoping for more than a touch.

With his crush on a river of lost ships
all was possible, bursting with smells.
He was hoping for more than a touch,
received less than an airborne kiss.

All was possible. Bursting with smells
of the shore. He had planned for love
received less than an airborne kiss,
no more than a smudge in the margins

of the shore. He had planned for love
to power the turbine blades, but
no more than a smudge in the margins
would propel the journey backwards.

To power the turbine blades, but
how? Who was he now? What scent
would propel the journey backwards,
into the cave of our father's lost youth?

How? Who was he now? What scent
did he touch in the creases of her blouse?
Into the cave of our father's lost youth,
a fever that bled into stars.

Did he touch, in the creases of her blouse,
our father's missing memories
a fever that bled into stars,
book-fishing with his sister on a ship?

Brorealism

They say inside each bro is a different
identical bro, and inside that bro is the chicken
that laid the egg that started the world,
but dude, where's your magnetic pocket knife,
your heliotropic brain extensions made
for the afterlife, you know, your poetry?
When will you let your mouth become
the gap between the pizza crust and the cheese,
when will the earth become a ping-pong-ball-
sized pupil bopping past the forest of liquid
gold yolk-filled Solo cups and into the firmament?
You may be a bro, but that doesn't mean your
soul can't leak glitter all over the baseball diamond.
You may be a guy, but that doesn't mean
your liver doesn't wear a pink feather beret,
that your id isn't draped in metallic negligee.
If inside each suburb is an identical suburb
where McMansions hide teeming cities
within, then when will your living room
explode into grimy, kaleidoscopic subways,
into cracked beakers full of the ashes of
interplanetary love affairs? In Brorealism,
none of us knows shit and that is the shit.
Even if the moonlight is made of cell phone
flashlights, even if the closet full of broken
telescope top hats is covered by a rack of
faded beer-label caps. Even if your vocabulary
is shrinking into atomic sub-particles,
please put down your TV-shaped bong.
Try opening that hole in your ear.

Wrap It in a Beehive

All I want to do is stay
home, flirt with my baby
sister's babysitter, admire
my reflection in my
mother's butcher knife
and stuff my chowhole
with sweet potato fries,
but then there's that ho
again, throwing down
that flaxen mane from
her window in the sky,
throwing around an
aromatic daffodil-shaped
cloud of amorous vapor
which envelops the world
and makes me forget
my true bro-ness. I know
they say her heart is made
of steel, but her lips taste
like stone fruit trifle
and her armpits smell
like places I don't admit
to her I've been. (Cue
the flutes.) So when
I hear the sound of her
braids swaying in the wind,
and the squeaky rattle
of her chained-up thighs,
like old-fashioned birdsongs
wooing me with their noisy
charms, my limbs start
to scale her hair, until
my palms are rough
and my fingers are fire-
engine red, and I don't
even mind the blisters.

Self-Portrait with Missing B Movie

Don't tell me that your runaway daughter
has drained the color from your television set

or that the creature from Planet X has removed
your Facebook, replaced your Instagram avatar

with a picture of his claw. None of these
is an excuse for magnifying the true you.

From the depths of the sea, there's always
that wired jar with the brain that won't die,

or some clone named Joanna who keeps
swallowing the same glob of nuclear fallout.

Listen to the oracle whose mouth opens
and closes all night long. Between the towers

of empty bottles of Coca-Cola and congealed
neon grilled cheese, try to hide your face

like the naked woman with the glow-in-the-dark
UFO mask. Finally accept that the Serpent Boy

has terrorized your failing planet long enough.
Start again as a giant gorilla or radioactive squid.

Live young, die like an action hero at a sauna.
Sing with all twenty of your sexual organs ablaze.

Solar Alert

We were proud of our newborn worlds.
You pushed Mars in a heat-resistant stroller,
and I slung infant Earth in a pink Björn.

In those days, single moms were not in style.
No one took our picture for *Galaxy Today*
or helped us pump milk into zero-G bottles.

Still, we had fun. While the kids orbited,
we gossiped about our sulking nemesis,
filled black hole cupcakes with pudding.

Soon our progeny wanted more than childhood
could provide. Saturn slipped away first.
Her mother discovered her texting pictures

of her bare rings. Then Venus was caught
stealing a rock from Alpha Centauri. You worried
that Neptune never left his dank bedroom,

that his goth poetry about killer bunny rabbits
signaled a belief in the multiverse. Being a mom
was harder than being a god, so we took up

red wine and online shopping, stopped bragging
about our budding globes, maxed out our credit cards
on psychoanalysis, fair-trade chocolate and clogs.

Funicular

We twist around thin mountains
and skyscrapers in a rickety tram.

Hanging from a wire, we float
over warehouses and lavender pagodas.

I'm not scared, but a little airsick
when the car lurches, starts to rock.

The wind lifts up   the crooked hem
of my linen dress   the edges
of the trees blurring,

and yes, the man and two women
with me are just *temporary* friends.

The man, like me, is aging
one year   per minute.

As we talk, his eyebrow hair   turns gray
and the lines   on his face expand
like spider webs.

The women grow younger slowly.
Their hips become narrower.

Shimmering with the afterglow
of afternoon sex and unsweetened ice tea,
they smell like the memory of being born.

One lusts after the older man.

          She would want him if only he weren't
sleeping with so-and-so—
          that teenager with the body
of a teenager.

I am, of course, disgusted,
but what can I say?

I thought I was flirting, realize now

        that I have become too old
for anyone to love.

As I think this,   the wire holding the tram up
splits,   but I'm okay,   not really afraid.

I feel an odd calm,
                and on a warm current of air,

we drift slowly toward   the ocean, and I listen

        to what sounds like the lullaby
        of a fragrant tangerine
        played with a bow as if it were a violin.

I think of time as an arrow
        bent in a circle, and this image
        fills me with a new kind of joy.

Finally in slow motion   we land
on a white sand beach.

Our legs are unsteady,

                and everything is silent,

the dragon back of the city
        fading into clouds.

I Have a Secret Crush on Everyone in the World

When I say I have a secret crush on everyone
in the world, I mean the earth is a fur-covered
fireball, speeding into the expanding spaces
between paragliding atoms. It means I have
a crush on the way your dangling earlobes
say one thing and your elephant, anxious
hips say another—the way you dial the same
number six times before you build up the nerve
to finish. And yes, it means I am seriously
crushing on your chipped gold nail polish,
the way it signifies a desire to make the world
more beautiful, but also the way it displays
a fuck-you approach to beauty. I was going
to email to say I have a crush on your pre-
apocalyptic recipe poems, but it's 2018
and according to Twitter only old folks
use email. Is there anything more crush-
worthy than a manifesto spelled out in
lightly frosted snickerdoodles, or an essay
floating in a lagoon-shaped swimming pool?
I have a public crush on the number 8 bus,
alfresco Thai brunches and dirty Brooklyn
swans. I love all errors and eras equally.
I have a repressed crush on New Jersey
pollution, the way its oil refineries remind
me I have a nose. To have a crush is to crush
out doubt so thoroughly its green, leathery
skin becomes your own, to taste another's
DNA so purely Januaries dissolve into vats
of frothy vanilla egg creams, spilling into
the cracks of your spine and your loose brain
jelly, into old feet and the cold twitch of your
jaw. To crush is to slide into the neural network
where our wires are made of birdsongs
and magenta-colored loss, is to feel the floor
open and the reverberating metallic shivers after.

History Lesson

The first coins were made
of glass so we could look
through them, glimpse our lives
before the invention of money.

We could see the pond
we used to watch goldfish
bubble in and the mud
that covered our feet in July.

We didn't miss the language of blinks,
the way value was a dance
choreographed by branches in wind.

We missed our lives in the fields,
in the dirt, with the seals on the rocks
who knew our names and could
retell our dreams in barks.

After the era of hard cash ended,
we survived by bartering hugs,
made new credit cards out
of discarded contact lenses
and swiped raw guilt out
of our tightening stomachs.

My mother would say,
"Before you were born,
we didn't need objects to be happy.

There was no such thing
as *things*—it was just *us*,
floating between pages of air."

The Adjunct Commuter (A Cento)

Over the shrill echoes,
I saw the bus.

Now-ness and then-ness.
          A thud. A thump.

Out of the ruins of the clock:
a freight train in your chest,
giddy mishaps of blackness.

Submission to the submachine,
the wind's dramatic flesh.

Air in air. I clomp clomp.

Wheels are inside me thundering.
Minutes shine at the tips of branches.

Hair caught on a bus thrown back

At the edge of the world, silent flashes
escaping from time.

The wind cries like a wounded animal.
A bird's metallic voice.

          So what about those many
sheets of drifting time?

The caravans left.

The traffic signal sways.

Through the chambers of the eye,
                    the street's beaten gray.
                    air sped by.

A south wind carrying fangs, sunflowers,
alphabets.

The red minute waits.
Green just lies there a while breathing.

Everything comes bearing a new name.
I see daylight take off running,

Face to the wind's teeth.

Acknowledgments

Versions of the poems appeared in the following journals. I am grateful to the editors.

Across the Margin: "Hexagon," "Brorealism" and "Crunch!"

Another Chicago Magazine: "Funicular"

Apogee Magazine: "Still Life with Island," "I Have a Secret Crush on Everyone in the World," "Boredom" and "History Lesson"

The Awl: *"Mauve Decade"*

Barrow Street: "Solar Alert"

Battery Journal: "The Poetry Reading," "Are We Having Fun Yet?" and "Benediction for a New Year"

Boog City:"Justin Bieber Visits the Anne Frank House" and "Lines from Brooklyn Fortune Cookies"

Brooklyn Rail: "The Adjunct Commuter," "The Adjunct Commuter (A Cento)," "Lavender" and "Kerosene"

Crab Creek Review: "History Lesson"

Conduit: "To a New Era"

Diode: "Whiskers"

Eleven, Eleven: "Margaret Thatcher Dies the Same Day Neruda's Bones Are Exhumed"

Fence: "Search Engine Overlord "

Hanging Loose: "November," " "Listen to What I'm Saying, not What I Say" "Semifreddo, "Who Else Should I Not Trust with Language?" "Foster Avenue," "Self-Portrait with B Movie," and "The B Train"

Homestead Review: " Household Tips for a New Era"

Journal of New Jersey Poets: "Broken Singularity, Kali Tribe Sestina" "A Short Essay on Middle Age" and "The Adjunct Commuter"

La Vague: "In the Spleen of the City"

Posit: "President's Day"and "Self-Portrait as Poem Or This Tyger Burns the Bones of William Blake"

Pretty Owl: "Why the Symmetry of a Bagel Is an Atheist Prayer"

Positive Magnets: "Song of the Rooster"

New Orleans Review: "Why Can't Middle Age Be Like Childhood, But with Sex, Liquor and Hipper Boots?"

New American Writing: "Moveable Us" and "Old Weather"

Marsh Hawk Review: "History Lesson"

Ping Pong: "Breaker"

Saint Ann's Review: "Muriel Said That to Be a Jew in the 20th Century Is to Be Offered a Gift."

Speech is Not Free: "A Short Essay on Protest"

SurVision Magazine: "Not True/False but Quality-Controlled Red-State Picaresque," and "Listen to What You Cannot Hear"

White Whale Review: "Wrap It in a Beehive"

And the anthologies:

The Dia Poetry Anthology, The Dia Foundation
Dream Closet, Steerage Press
Brooklyn Poets Anthology, Brooklyn Arts Press
Like Light: 25 Years of Poetry & Prose, Bright Hill Press
What Rough Beast, Indolent Books

Videos of some of the poems have appeared in *Battery, Requited Journal, Moving Poems Journal* and *Triquarterly.*

"Are We Having Fun Yet?" was written for the DoubleTake series at Apex Art

Also, thanks to Anne Noonan, who designed and printed a broadside of "History Lesson" for my reading at the Shed in Park Slope, Brooklyn.

Special thank you to my dear friends (and husband) who offered support and suggestions on these poems:

Martine Bellen, Thomas Devaney, Elaine Equi, Boni Joi, Bob Kerr, Sharon Mesmer, Jean-Paul Pecqueur, Lauren Russell, Lisa Shea, Yerra Sugarman

And thank you to Caroline Hagood and Dick Lourie for expert editing.

I am also very grateful to my students for inspiration. And to all of the editors at Hanging Loose for so many years of encouragement.